WILD *at* HEART

THE COUPLE'S GUIDE

Discovering the Secret of a Man's Soul

JOHN ELDREDGE

THOMAS NELSON

Since 1798

NASHVILLE   DALLAS   MEXICO CITY   RIO DE JANEIRO   BEIJING

Published in Nashville, Tennessee, by Thomas Nelson. Thomas Nelson is a trademark of Thomas Nelson, Inc.

Published in association with Yates & Yates, www.yates2.com

Thomas Nelson, Inc., titles may be purchased in bulk for educational, business, fund-raising, or sales promotional use. For information, please e-mail SpecialMarkets@ThomasNelson.com.

Unless otherwise noted, Scripture quotations are taken from the HOLY BIBLE: NEW INTERNATIONAL VERSION®. © 1973, 1978, 1984 by International Bible Society. Used by permission of Zondervan Publishing House. All rights reserved.

Scripture quotations marked NKJV are from THE NEW KING JAMES VERSION. © 1982 by Thomas Nelson, Inc. Used by permission. All rights reserved.

Scripture quotations marked NLT are from the *Holy Bible*, New Living Translation. © 1996. Used by permission of Tyndale House Publishers, Inc., Wheaton, Illinois 60189. All rights reserved.

Scripture quotations marked NASB are from the NEW AMERICAN STANDARD BIBLE®, © The Lockman Foundation 1960, 1962, 1963, 1968, 1971, 1972, 1973, 1975, 1977, 1995. Used by permission. (www.Lockman.org)

Portions of this text are adapted from the *Wild at Heart Field Manual*.

ISBN 1-4002-8072-9
ISBN 978-1-4002-8072-8

Printed in the United States of America

09 10 11 12 RRD 6 5 4 3 2 1

How to Use the Study Guides as a Couple

The messages in *Wild at Heart* and *Captivating* have helped millions of men and women discover the secret of the masculine and feminine hearts. Now, with the study guide you hold in your hand, that life-changing discovery is something you can share with your significant other. In the pages that follow, you'll find questions, exercises, and journaling space that coordinate with *Wild at Heart*.

Here's what we recommend for using this as a couple:

1) Read *Wild at Heart* while your partner reads *Captivating*

2) After each chapter, process your experience and thoughts in this study guide

3) Then, after you've both completed a chapter in your book and the corresponding study guide chapter, set some time aside to share with each other what you are learning, what discoveries you're making.

It's a simple process that will lead to a deep understanding of yourself *and* your partner. Without a doubt, you will both be astounded by the level of intimacy that can come from intentional sharing prompted by the message in these books!

CONTENTS

INTRODUCTION

You are standing on the brink of what could be the greatest adventure you've ever known . . . and your fiercest battle.

When it comes to the story of your life and how it will be told ages hence around the campfires of the kingdom, the central chapter will be your masculine journey. That journey is the essential quest of your life, whereby you recover your true heart, discover your real name, and find your place in the battle. Everything else flows from there.

It's hard. It's scary. And it's worth it.

There is a life that few men know . . . a life so rich and free, so dangerous and yet so exhilarating in its impact that if you knew now what you *could* have, you would sell everything to find it. But you have a sense of it even now, from the echoes in your heart, the hints in your deepest desires, the Voice that has been calling you for a long time.

I'm proud of you. It took guts to get this far, and you are about to enter an elite company of men. This will be a major turning point in your life—maybe *the* turning point. Behind is the life you've led; ahead lies your destiny.

You'll notice we didn't call this a "workbook" or a "curriculum." You're embarking on a journey, not doing your homework. Approach it like that. Take your time; find your stride. You're not memorizing answers; you're reclaiming your *heart*.

You're going to experience a lot of different emotions, and hear a lot of thoughts as you go through this. Things like, *I don't have time to get to this right now* or *This may be for other guys, but not for me* or *I'm just a poser*. About 99 percent of that is from the Enemy. He fears what will happen if you take this journey. Fight those thoughts and emotions, and press on.

At some point, you'll want your woman to read *Wild at Heart*, too. Every woman I've spoken to has loved it. Besides, this is so revolutionary, she needs to have a clue about what you're up to and why you're suddenly acting the way you are.

There are many in the great cloud of witnesses cheering for you. I am one of them.

—JOHN

CHAPTER I

WILD AT HEART

The spiritual life cannot be made suburban. It is always frontier, and we who live in it must accept and even rejoice that it remains untamed.

—HOWARD MACEY

This chapter isn't about fixing or solving anything . . . including you. Instead, I merely want to *awaken* something. I want to arouse that masculine heart that so often slumbers down under the surface of your life. I want to give it permission to come out of hiding and give you some clarity and, more important, *validation* for this heart that beats so deep within you. Your journey starts there.

Men and women bear the image of God either *as men* or *as women*. There is, therefore, something deep and true and universal to the masculine heart. And it's been lost—or better, driven into hiding. To get your masculine heart back, you cannot begin with more duty and obligation. You must begin with your deepest desires. *What makes you come alive?* Somewhere down in your heart are three core desires: a battle to fight, an adventure to live, and a beauty to rescue.

What has God set in the masculine heart? More important, what has he set in *your* masculine heart? I believe that the movies you love are a clue to your heart, to what makes you come alive. So let's start there. Write down a handful of movies that have stirred your heart over the years. And from those stories, what roles, what heroes would you love to play?

Another way of getting below the surface, to *real* desires of our hearts, is to look at what we do with our free time. Let's say you have three months of vacation coming up, a sabbatical all to yourself, and plenty of cash to bankroll it. Where would you go? What would you do?

Looking back now at the movies you love, the roles you'd want to play, and your three-month daydream, what does it tell you about your own heart? What are you made for?

A BATTLE TO FIGHT

Remember back into your boyhood for a moment. Did you play games involving battles? Cowboys and Indians, perhaps, or maybe cops and robbers? What were they?

Who were your boyhood heroes? An army man, an athlete, or maybe a cowboy, a superhero like Batman or Superman? Did they have a great battle to fight?

Look back now at your favorite movies you jotted down. What is the hero's great battle? Which of those battles would *you* love to fight, if you were him?

This longing may have submerged from years of neglect, and a man may not feel that he is up to the battles he knows await him. But the desire is there. Every man wants to play the hero. I find that many men have long buried their desire to be a hero. But isn't there something in you that wants to be applauded, cheered for what you've done? What debate would you love to win, what deal would you love to land, what "big fish" would you love to catch, what hill would you love to take?

What happens in you when you watch one of those powerful stories such as *Braveheart* or *Flying Tigers* or *Top Gun*? Is there anything in a great battle scene that stirs your heart? Can you sense something fierce down there?

What if a terrorist broke into your house tonight and threatened the lives of your wife and children—would you simply let it happen? If you were armed, would you use your weapon? Do you sense something fierce in your own heart now?

Have you ever been told that fierceness is a *good* thing?

ADVENTURE

I'm convinced that adventure, with all its requisite danger and wildness, is a deeply spiritual longing written into the soul of man. Does that surprise you, hearing that adventure is a *spiritual* longing given to us by God?

What were some of the "great adventures" you had—or dreamed of or read about—as a boy?

Describe an adventure you've had in more recent years, a time when you really came alive. What did it require of you?

ON WILDERNESS

Eve was created within the lush beauty of Eden's garden. But Adam, if you'll remember, was created *outside* the garden, in the wilderness. Only afterward was he brought to Eden. And ever since then boys have never been at home indoors, and men have an insatiable longing to explore. We long to return to the outdoors; it's when most men come alive. Have you ever spent time in the outdoors? Did you enjoy it?

Look at the heroes of the biblical text. Moses does not encounter the living God at the mall. He finds him (or is found by him) somewhere out in the deserts of Sinai, a long way from the comforts of Egypt. The same is true of Jacob, who has his wrestling match with God not on the living room sofa but in a wadi in Mesopotamia. Where did the great prophet Elijah go to recover his spiritual strength? To the wild. As did John the Baptist, and his cousin, Jesus, who was *led by the Spirit* into the wilderness.

The early Celtic Christians called the Holy Spirit the Wild Goose. They knew that following him meant accepting a great adventure. Has the Spirit ever led you into the wilderness—a calling, or a haunting to just "get away from it all," get out into the wild? If he did so now, would you go?

Adventure *requires* something of us, puts us to the test. Though we may fear the test, at the same time we yearn to be tested, to discover that we have what it takes. Have you ever seen, in your desires or even in your fantasies, something "wild" (risky, adventurous, undomesticated) in your own heart?

Have you understood that wildness to be a good thing? Would you like there to be a wildness about you?

A BEAUTY TO RESCUE

A man wants to be the hero to the Beauty. It's not enough to be a hero; it's that he is a hero *to someone* in particular, to the woman he loves. Remember the first time you fell in love. Where did you meet? What was it about her that turned your head, captured your heart?

Think back again to the movie roles you'd love to play—who are the damsels you'd love to rescue?

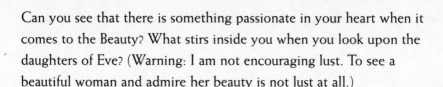

Can you see that there is something passionate in your heart when it comes to the Beauty? What stirs inside you when you look upon the daughters of Eve? (Warning: I am not encouraging lust. To see a beautiful woman and admire her beauty is not lust at all.)

Have you sensed that, at its core, your passion to rescue the Beauty is a good thing, part of your destiny?

ON EVE

The three desires of a woman's heart are to be fought for, to be invited up into a great adventure, and to unveil her beauty. What is your reaction to reading that? Can you see that now in what she loves and longs for?

Would you be willing to ask the Eve in your life about her desires? Ask her about her favorite movies and why she loves them. Ask her what she'd do with three months of vacation.

SOMETHING'S BEEN LOST

Corporate policies and procedures are designed with one aim: to harness a man to the plow and make him produce. How much room for your masculine soul—for adventure and battle and beauty—is there in your typical week?

The masculine heart needs a place where nothing is prefabricated. Where there is room for the soul. Where, finally, the geography around us corresponds to the geography of our hearts. How would you describe the "geography" of your daily world—does it fit the terrain of your deep heart?

Think about your life, your world. What do you feel pressure to be . . .

At home?

At work?

At church?

What would you say is the commonly held view in your church when it comes to a good Christian man?

SO WHERE DOES THAT LEAVE YOU?

There is the life we were *meant for* and the man we were *created to be* . . . and then there is the life we *have* and the man we *find ourselves* to be. They are often worlds apart. What is your great battle?

Where is your great adventure?

Who is the Beauty you are fighting for?

AN INVITATION—PERMISSION GRANTED

What if those deep desires in our hearts are telling us the truth, revealing to us the life we were *meant* to live? What might it look like for you to live from your "wild" heart?

On a scale of 1 to 10, how badly do you want to be a man living from your "wild" heart? Why'd you pick that number?

Take a moment now to speak to the Lord:

O Lord, open wide the eyes of my soul that I might see the true yearnings of my heart. Uncover my desire for adventure, battle, and beauty. Begin to dismantle all the messages that have challenged and assaulted your design of me. May your invitation to life as a man be forever before me. I accept the invitation to live from my deep heart. Father, use the words of this book and the meditations of my heart to guide, shape, and direct me in this journey that I might be the man you designed me to be. I ask this in the name of Jesus. Amen.

CHAPTER 2

THE WILD ONE WHOSE
IMAGE WE BEAR

How would telling people to be nice to one another get a man cruci-
fied? What government would execute Mister Rogers or Captain
Kangaroo?

—PHILIP YANCEY

Early in this chapter I said, "A man *has* to know where he comes from, and what he's made of." Those are two of the deepest questions of the masculine soul—even if we may not always be aware of them—and they are linked. What a man thinks he's made of is so often shaped by what he thinks his father is made of. Yet we are something more than our father's son . . . we bear the image of God. What does *that* mean? Perhaps in finding his wild heart we might find our own.

You must know where you come from, and what you're made of. But a father—even a good one—is never enough to fully and finally answer that question. This yearning for a battle to fight is deep in the heart of God. He, too, longs for adventure and risk—far more than we. And he has a Beauty to rescue, whom he pursues with amazing passion.

It would be helpful to take a moment or two to think about your father, the kind of man he is, or was. What was your father's occupation? What did he like to do?

11

What was he like emotionally? Was he serious? Did he have a good sense of humor?

How did he tend to deal with troubles and adversity?

What was your father's great battle or battles?

Would you say he was a man of deep courage? Was he fierce? Timid?

Was your father a man who lived life as a great adventure?

What was his courtship of your mother like? Have you seen him rescue the Beauty?

How would you characterize your father? Choose five or ten words that come to mind when you think of him as a man. Which of your father's attributes do you think you inherited?

Would it thrill you to be introduced as a "chip off the old block"? If not, can you think of a few words to describe the father you *wish* you had?

WHAT ABOUT JESUS?

It almost sounds too spiritual. In a man's search for his strength, telling him that he's made in the image of God may not sound like a whole lot of encouragement at first. To most men, God is either distant or he is weak—the very thing they'd report of their earthly fathers. Recall the words you used above to summarize your father. Which of those words feel true to you about God—especially as he relates to you?

And what about Jesus? . . . What is your image of Jesus as a *man*?

If you grew up in a religious home, can you recall some of the early pictures you saw of Jesus? Is he "gentle Jesus, meek and mild"? Or is he the fierce Lion of Judah?

You hear everyone at your church describe some guy as a "real godly man." What comes to mind about him?

What would you have to conclude about Jesus from the men in your church? For example, how do they handle controversy? Do they live with adventure? What have they done with the Beauty?

You can tell what kind of man you've got simply by noting the impact he has on you. Does he make you bored? Does he make you want to scream because he's just so very nice? . . . What do you feel *you* ought to do or be when you're around the men in your church?

"The Lord is a Gentleman." Have you heard that? Do you think it's accurate, as in, Is Jesus mostly concerned with good manners and with his reputation?

(Note: I want to draw a distinction between *nice* and *kind*. I'm using *nice* here to mean a passive, sweet, two-dimensional man who never, ever rocks the boat. But I don't mean to suggest that a godly man is therefore rude, or belligerent, or unable to be tender. Jesus could be fierce . . . or immensely kind, depending on what was needed.)

GOD'S BATTLE TO FIGHT

Remember that wild man, Samson? He's got a pretty impressive masculine résumé: killed a lion with his bare hands, pummeled and stripped thirty Philistines, and killed a thousand men with the jawbone of a donkey. Not a guy to mess with. Those events happened when *"the Spirit of the LORD came upon him"* (Judg. 15:14, emphasis added). How do you think a man would act if the Spirit of God got hold of him? Does Samson immediately come to mind? Why or why not?

When God delivers his people out of the bondage of Egypt, Pharaoh doesn't just roll over and take it. He sends his entire army on chariots to slaughter the fleeing slaves—including the women and children.

"Then the LORD said to Moses, 'Stretch out your hand over the sea so that the waters may flow back over the Egyptians and their chariots and horsemen' . . . and the LORD swept them into the sea. . . . the entire army of Pharaoh that had followed the Israelites . . . not one of them survived" (Ex. 14:26–28). It is after this battle that the Israelites cheered, "The LORD is a warrior" (Ex. 15:3).

This story from Exodus is just one among hundreds given to us in the Bible to reveal the warring activity of God. There are the great battles of King David, Jesus taking on the hypocrites, kicking out demons, and finally wrestling the keys of hell and death away from Satan. Would you gather from all this that God's nature is basically passive or aggressive?

And what *is* God's great battle to fight? Is it, as some churches seem to convey, simply to get people to stop sinning? What is God fighting *for*?

Read Revelation 19:11–21. How does Jesus bring an end to this chapter of his story?

GOD'S ADVENTURE TO LIVE

After God made this dangerous world, he pronounced it *good*. It's his way of letting us know he rather prefers adventure, danger, risk, the element of surprise. This whole creation is unapologetically wild. What do you learn about God's heart from a place like the outback of Australia?

We know he has a battle to fight—but does God have an *adventure* to live? Hasn't he got everything under absolute control? What have you been taught about the risk-taking nature of God?

On a scale of 1 to 10, rate your willingness to take risks (a) at work and (b) in your relationships.

Now, rate God's willingness to risk in his work and his relationships—keeping in mind the story from Genesis where God turns over the care of creation to Adam and Eve, and also gives them freedom to reject him, knowing that if they do, they'll plunge the whole world into evil.

And now recall that universal trait in little boys, who want to be the hero of some great and daring quest. Can you see something of the heart of God reflected there? (In saying that God has an adventure to live, I don't mean the world is chaotic, or out of control, or that somehow God's sovereignty is diminished. Far from it.)

GOD'S BEAUTY TO RESCUE

God's wildness and his fierceness are inseparable from his romantic heart. Would you say that God is *romantic?*

Whose idea was it to create the human form in such a way that a kiss could be so delicious? And he didn't stop there, as only lovers know. For some reason, most men never attribute the wonders of sex to God, that the whole delicious mystery of intercourse from foreplay to orgasm was his idea. But of course, it was.

Two questions: First, would such an erotic and scandalous book as Song of Songs have been placed in the Bible by the Christians *you* know? And second, what kind of God *would* put that book in the canon of holy Scripture?

Down through the centuries the church has understood the Song of Songs to be both a celebration of passion in marriage *and* a metaphor for Christ and his bride. Think about how much you want sex with a beautiful woman. How does *that* reflect the image of God?

God has a bride. What lengths will he go to in order to rescue her? For example, how long has he given pursuit?

THE INEVITABLE CONCLUSION

This is our true Father, the stock from which the heart of every man is drawn. From which *your* heart is drawn.

So often our word to boys is *don't*. Don't climb on that, don't be so aggressive, don't be so noisy, don't take such crazy risks. But God's design—which he placed in boys as the picture of himself—is a resounding *YES*. Be fierce, be wild, be passionate. Now what words would you use to describe a "godly man"?

Pray this prayer:

Lord, you are more passionate and more fierce than I ever imagined. Open my eyes, show me your true nature, and show me your nature in me. I want your work in my life—O make me free, alive to fight the battles you bring me, to live the adventure, to rescue the beauty. Do this work in my soul, I pray, dear Christ. Amen.

CHAPTER 3

THE QUESTION THAT HAUNTS EVERY MAN

The tragedy of life is what dies inside a man while he lives.

—ALBERT SCHWEITZER

This chapter takes you into some naked self-assessment. Something's gone wrong in men, and we know it. Something about us, or in us, is just not what we know it was meant to be. What's *happened* to us? Why aren't we more fierce, daring, and passionate? You're going to need to be brutally honest if you hope to continue the journey from here. Remember, we have to cross the desert, the no-man's-land, before winning the promised land.

The world is filled with caricatures of masculinity—posers—but very few real men. And every one of us posers shares a deepest fear: to be found out, exposed as an impostor. The reason, in part, goes back to Adam's fall—and the way every man since him has fallen. So men handle that by becoming either violent (driven) or retreating (passive)—we mishandle our strength.

A man is fierce . . . passionate . . . wild at heart? You wouldn't know it from what normally walks around in a pair of trousers. If that's true, how come there are so many lonely women, so many fatherless children, so few *men* around? How come when men look in their hearts they don't discover something valiant and dangerous? Most of the time I feel more fearful than I do fierce. Why is that?

OUR STRUGGLES

Without a great battle in which a man can live and die, the fierce part of our nature goes underground and just sort of stews there in anger that seems to have no reason. Are you aware of a simmering anger down under the surface of your life? Describe a recent event that really hacked you off. What happened?

Anger is not necessarily a bad thing, by the way. Paul says, "Be angry, and do not sin" (Eph. 4:26 NKJV), which makes it clear that it's possible to be angry in a righteous way. Furthermore, I think anger is a good sign—at least there's something still alive inside, something that would love to fight back.

Why are so many men addicted to sports? It's the biggest adventure many of us ever taste. Why do so many others lose themselves in their career? Same reason. Where do you go for a taste of adventure these days? What might the balance on your credit cards say about where you are looking for adventure?

Where do you feel *pulled* to go for a thrill, even if you haven't given in?

What about lust—how's it going there? And when is your struggle with lust the strongest? Can you connect it to disappointment, stress, or pressure at work or at home?

We will never get past our struggles and addictions until we recover the true heart and true life we were meant for.

OUR FEAR

Because we bear the image of God in our strength we are made to *come through*. And yet we wonder, *Can I? Will I? When the going gets rough, when it really matters, can I really pull it off?* That is why every man shares the same core fear of being exposed, being "found out." It's time for some candid self-assessment. How do you measure up as a man? Be honest—no more, no less.

Let's take the battle: How well are you fighting these days? Do you live with courage for the most part?

What battles do you *not* want to face?

If you were called into a real battle tomorrow, would you step forward to lead the charge, knowing beyond a doubt that you *are* powerful and dangerous?

How about real adventure: are you living with risk and daring, or do you play it safe more often than not?

Write a list of "my worst fears." Why do you fear them?

And as for the Beauty—are you fighting for her heart? How often do you talk to her at an intimate level? Do you often ask her how she thinks the two of you are doing? Have you *ever* asked her that?

Really—how do you see yourself as a man? Are words like *strong, passionate,* and *dangerous* words you would choose?

Do you have the courage to ask those in your life what *they* think of you as a man? What words do you fear *they* would choose?

Okay, I have a mission for you. But it may be the bravest thing you've ever done . . . . and the most life-changing. Ask a few people who know you well—your wife, your older children, a friend or colleague—to give you some feedback about you *as a man*. It's hard to get an honest and candid reply. You might explain that you're working through some frank self-assessment, and ask them to answer you in writing. (For the woman in your life, you may ask, for example, "What am I like to live with? Do you feel invited to share your heart with me? Do you feel pursued by me—that I am truly fighting for you?")

ADAM AND HIS SONS

God gave Adam a noble mission, a mission that is still written into the heart of every man, in the form of his desires. What is that mission, in your own words?

Was that a new revelation to you—that Adam was standing right there when Eve was being tempted, and *he didn't do a thing*? How did that strike you?

Does Adam's sin help you understand the way men nowadays sin— and, more important, can you see that same dynamic working in your own life? When have you been silent when you really should have spoken up?

AND EVE?

Your woman is fallen as well, of course. We all are. But women sin differently from men. They tend to hide their vulnerability and become hard, or independent, or controlling women—or they become desperately needy and overly submissive. How does your woman handle her vulnerability?

What about her beauty—does she hide it behind efficiency and working hard and being "spiritual"? Or perhaps she handles her insecurity there by trying extra hard, . . . talking a lot about her weight and the like. Is *alluring* a word that characterizes your woman most of the time?

How strong do you feel when your wife is not doing well, or when you are faced with her sin? Do you feel like a man around her?

POSERS

Adam (and every man with him) has blown it, and he knows that something has gone wrong within him, that he is no longer what he was meant to be. It's not just that he makes a bad decision; he *gives away* something essential to his nature. Then what happens? Adam hides. "I was afraid because I was naked, so I hid" (Gen. 3:10). Understand that verse, let its implications sink in, and the men around you will suddenly come into focus. We are hiding, every last one of us. Desperately afraid of exposure, terrified of being seen for what we are and *are not*, we have run off into the bushes. We hide in our office, at the gym, . . . and mostly *behind our personality*. Describe your personality.

What is it you are afraid people are going to see about you as a man?

I offered two basic categories for how a fallen man handles his strength: violent men and retreating men. Violent men are *striving* in various ways to prove that they are a man, or at least, to never be exposed. Retreating men basically live to avoid the question and stay away from any possible exposure. Which of the two categories do you put yourself in, and why? Can you give a few examples (from home and from work)?

Adam and Eve's fall sent a tremor through the human race. A fatal flaw entered the original, and it's been passed on to every son and daughter. Even if he can't quite put it into words, every man is haunted by the question, "Am I really a man? Have I got what it takes . . . when it counts?" Are you a bit more aware now of that Question in your own heart and life?

Search me, O God, and know my heart. Reveal to me the ways I pose and hide. May I live with passion and zeal; may my soul be captured by you for something big, noble, and worthy of your kingdom. Free me to be a strong, passionate, and dangerous man as you created me to be. Draw me beyond the battles I know I can win, lure me to larger adventures speak with power those words I long to hear: "You have what it takes." I ask all this in Jesus' name. Amen.

CHAPTER 4
THE WOUND

Little Billy's mother was always telling him exactly what he was allowed to do and what he was not allowed to do. All the things he was allowed to do were boring. All the things he was not allowed to do were exciting. One of the things he was NEVER, NEVER allowed to do, the most exciting of them all, was to go out through the garden gate all by himself and explore the world beyond.

—ROALD DAHL, *The Minpins*

Your goal is simple, but daunting: to uncover your wound. You need to see how you've been wounded, understand where the wound came from, and how it has shaped the way you've lived every day of your life—right up to this moment today.

Every boy has two Questions: Do I have what it takes? Am I powerful? Most men live their lives haunted by the Question, or crippled by the answer they've been given. Because masculinity is *bestowed*. A boy learns who he is and what he's got from a man, or the company of men. Yet every boy, in his journey to become a man, takes an arrow in the center of his heart, in the place of strength. And the wound is nearly always given by his father. With the wound comes a message, and out of the message we make a vow. The result is a false self—a deep uncertainty in the soul, and a driven or passive man on the outside.

UNDERSTANDING THE MASCULINE JOURNEY

The plan from the beginning of time was that his father would lay the foundation for a young boy's heart, and pass on to him that essential knowledge and confidence in his strength. Dad would be the first man in his life, and forever the most important man. Above all, he would answer the Question for his son and give him his name. Describe a time in your life when you heard words like those Jesus heard from his Father—"I am deeply proud of you; you have what it takes."

Would you say that your father or another key man, or perhaps the company of men, "actively intervened" on your behalf in order to tell you who you are as a man? Give an example. Was that example an exception?

Over the course of your youth up to young manhood, what were you rewarded for, delighted in because of? Did that really answer The Question for you?

How has life answered The Question for you? Describe it.

MOTHERS AND SONS

It would be good to explore your relationship with your mother before moving on to Dad more deeply. After all, a boy is brought into the world by his mother, and she is the center of his universe in those first tender months and years. Describe your relationship with your mother? Was it closer than your relationship with your father? Answer that question for three main phases of boyhood:

preschool years (ages 0–5)

grade school (ages 6–12)

middle school and high school (ages 13–18)

Was your mother a source of mercy and tenderness for you? (This would be a *good* thing, by the way.)

Did your mother allow you to be "dangerous"? Did she let you ride your bike with no hands? Jump off the high dive?

There comes a time in every young man's life when he leaves his mother's side and enters the world of men, starting with his father's world. Did your mom let you go willingly? Did she make it difficult? Did she even understand?

What is your relationship like with her today, compared to your relationship with your dad?

FROM FATHER TO SON

Masculinity is an *essence* that is hard to articulate but that a boy naturally craves just as he craves food and water. It is something passed between men. What are some of your favorite memories together with your dad? *Why* are they favorite memories?

My boys love to wrestle with me. They love the physical contact, to brush against my cheek, feel the sandpaper of my whiskers, my strength all around them, and to test theirs on me. Did you wrestle with your dad? Was there regular, warm contact with him?

Are you comfortable being physically affectionate with your children?

What did your father teach you to do when you were a boy? Describe what he passed along to you in several arenas:

Sports

Fighting/self-defense

Women

Finances

God

How would you sum up your father's "life lesson" to you?

THE FATHER-WOUND

Because wounds are rarely discussed and even more rarely healed, every man carries a wound. And the wound is nearly always given by his father.

I need to clarify two things when it comes to finding our "wound." First, it is not necessarily one clear wound, given on an unforgettable day you remember in detail. Second, no matter how good a man your father was, and may still be, he is not Jesus Christ. Every father is a son of Adam. What *is* your wound? Do you remember how it was given?

And what was the *message* of that wound—or that series of wounds?

In the case of violent fathers, the boy's Question is answered in a devastating way. Violent fathers give a wound that is easier to recognize. How did you experience your father's anger?

The passive wounds are not as obvious. Passive fathers give a blow that is harder to define, because it came as an absence.

If you still have no clue as to what your wound might be, go to the *effect* of the wound and work backward. Do you live each day with a deep inner strength that comes from knowing you are a real man? Or are you a driven man, or a passive man? When did that feeling of drivenness or passivity set in?

Another way of getting at the wound is by asking yourself what you are currently working hard at not being discovered as. What arenas are you staying comfortably away from? Why—where did that originate?

THE WOUND'S EFFECT

By now you have some idea of the impact your wound has had upon your masculine heart. . . . We take a wound, and with it comes a message, a lie about us and about the world and often about God, too. The wound and lie then lead to a vow, a resolution to never, ever do again whatever it was that might have brought the wound. From that vow we develop a false self.

$$\frac{\text{Wound}}{\text{Lie}} \quad + \quad \text{Vow} \quad = \quad \text{False Self}$$

Example:

$$\frac{\text{My father left}}{\text{"You are on your own"}} \quad + \quad \begin{array}{c} \text{I will never trust} \\ \text{anyone again} \end{array} \quad = \quad \begin{array}{c} \text{A very independent,} \\ \text{driven man} \end{array}$$

Can you remember making a sort of vow when you were younger—maybe after being wounded? What was that vow?

Can you see that vow affecting you today? How?

So many men feel stuck—either paralyzed and unable to move, or unable to stop moving. Which would you say is true of you these days?

ONE FINAL QUESTION

What *would* you have loved to hear from your father?

If your father bestowed a clear sense of masculinity upon you, give great thanks to God for having blessed you with a father who gave to you what so few have had. Ask God to carry you on in your masculine journey. If your father didn't bestow a masculine blessing on you, take some time now to lay that before God.

O God, it's true. My heart is wounded within me. Come to me, dear Jesus, speak to my heart such strong and sure words, affirm my masculinity, and grant me the ears to hear you speak those life-giving words. Take me now on the journey of my heart's recovery. Be my guide every step. In your name I pray. Amen.

CHAPTER 5

THE BATTLE FOR A MAN'S HEART

To give a man back his heart is the hardest mission on earth.
—FROM THE MOVIE *Michael*

The goal of this chapter is to see the emasculation you've endured, to uncover the famished craving you have for validation, and to reveal where you've taken that craving in hopes of an answer. The reason is that we're about to seek the answer God has for us, but it cannot come and we cannot understand his way with us until we see clearly where we've taken our hearts.

The assault on a man continues through his life, and its effect is emasculation. That assault is far more premeditated that most of us thought. The result is a famished craving in the soul—our desperate desire for validation as a man. We take our search many places, but eventually we all take it to the Woman.

Nearly every blow falls in the same place—as an attack on a man's strength. Can you recall assaults you've endured over the years? What about at school? Were you taunted on the playground?

What about your friends? Have they been loyal and affirming?

41

And at work—are you honored there as a man of strength? Are you invited to speak your mind feely? What price have you paid for job security?

How about church—have you been validated as a powerful warrior there? What happens to people who rock the boat?

What about in marriage? Does your wife *encourage* you to be dangerous, to seek adventure, to take risks? Give an example or two.

In what ways does she intentionally arouse you, seduce you with her feminine beauty and affirm you as a man?

The world is unnerved by a truly masculine man, and so it tries to socialize men *away* from all that is fierce and wild and passionate. Yet God made men the way they are because we *need* them to be the way they are. I cited the safety of a neighborhood, or the bringing down of slavery, or the men who gave their places on the lifeboats of the *Titanic*. Can you name a few more examples of where the nature of men is exactly what the world has *needed*?

What might be different in your world if *you* were far more dangerous? And, who in your life is encouraging you to be that way?

WHAT'S REALLY GOING ON HERE, ANYWAY?

Take a look around you. What do you see in the lives of the men that you work with, live by, go to church alongside? Are they full of passionate freedom? Do they fight well? Are their women deeply grateful for how well their men have loved them?

I said that this is a battlefield, that we are at war, that in fact we are in the late stages of the long and vicious war against the human heart. Does that sound a bit too dramatic for you? What *have* you understood the situation to be?

Have you ever conceived of Life as a *war*?

What have your wounds prevented you from doing in your life? Have you followed your dreams?

The wounds we've taken were leveled against us with stunning accuracy. Did it occur to you that all those wounds were aimed, that they were not random but *intentional*? Does it seem to make a bit more sense now?

The Enemy fears you. You are dangerous big-time. If you ever really got your heart back, lived it with courage, you would do a lot of damage . . . on the side of Good. You *can* get your heart back. But if you want your heart back, if you want the wound healed and your strength restored and to find your true name, *you're going to have to fight for it.* Does not something in you stir a little, a yearning to live? And doesn't another voice rush in, urging caution, maybe wanting to dismiss me altogether? Do you see the Battle in your reaction?

OUR SEARCH FOR AN ANSWER

The bottom line is this: We still need to know what we never heard, or heard so badly, from our fathers. *We need to know* who we are and if we have what it takes. What do we do now with that ultimate question? Where do we go to find an answer? In order to help you find the answer to The Question, let me ask you another: What *have* you done with your question? Where have you taken it? You see, a man's core question does not go away. It is a hunger so essential to our souls that it will compel us to find a resolution. In truth, it drives everything we do. Do you see it driving you? In what ways?

Another way of asking this is, what would it feel like death to lose, or to know you will *never, ever* attain?

Where does most of the energy of your life get spent in a normal week? And why are you spending it there?

TAKING IT TO EVE

I confessed my long and sad story of searching for "the woman that will make me feel like a man," how I went from girlfriend to girlfriend trying to get an answer to my Question, that I was certain that being the Hero to the Beauty would bring me validation as a man. What has been your history with women? Start with your first love, your first sweetheart, and go right up to the present, including your wife or current relationship. Then, answer the following questions for each woman:

Who pursued whom?

What was the relationship like? Was it stormy, passionate, boring?

Who initiated phone calls, chose what you'd do on a date, basically provided the energy behind the relationship? Did that change over time?

How did she make you feel about yourself as a man?

Who broke up with whom? How was it done . . . and why? What was the message to you?

What were you looking for from her? Do you see the way you took your Question to her?

Notice the flow of all your relationships—do you see a pattern emerging?

Is there a message about you as a man that has taken root?

By the way, this is why so many men secretly fear their wives. A wife sees her husband like no one else does . . . knows what he's made of. If he has given her the power to validate him as a man, then he has also given her the power to *invalidate* him, too. What grade do you feel you're currently getting from your woman? And what does that make you want to do?

THE GOLDEN-HAIRED WOMAN

Why is pornography more addictive for men than heroin? Because that seductive beauty reaches down inside and *touches your desperate hunger for validation as a man you didn't even know you had*. You must understand—this is deeper than legs and breasts and good sex. This may be the biggest revelation a man comes to about the Beauty—that his struggle with her is not about sex but about *validation*. Let me ask you now about the fantasy woman—the woman in your daydreams. How does she make you feel *as a man*?

Eve is a garden of delight (Songs 4:16). Man, oh man, is she! Femininity can really arouse masculinity—no question about it. But the answer to your Question can never, ever be found there. Has that ever really sunk in to you? Let it now. Just sit with this thought for a few minutes: *I will never find what I'm looking for in a woman*. What happens in your heart as you allow that to be true? Sadness? Relief?

Why have I said all this about our search for validation and the answer to our Question? Because we cannot hear the real answer until we see we've got a false one. As long as we chase the illusion, how can we face reality? If you take your question to Eve, it will break your heart. You can't get your answer there. In fact, you can't get your answer from any of the things men chase after to find their sense of self. There is only one source for the answer to your Question. And so no matter where you've taken your Question, you've got to take it back. You have to walk away. Will you? How . . . and when? What will you give up in order to find the Real Thing?

Father, I want to know You, but my coward heart fears to give up its toys. I cannot part with them without inward bleeding, and I do not try to hide from You the terror of the parting. I come trembling, but I do come. Please root from my heart all those things which I have cherished so long and which have become a very part of my living self, so that You may enter and dwell there without a rival. In Jesus' name. Amen. (A. W. Tozer, The Pursuit of God)

CHAPTER 6

THE FATHER'S VOICE

Who can give a man this, his own name?

—GEORGE MacDONALD

You have an opportunity now to completely reframe your relationship with God, where he becomes the one who is initiating you, taking you on the masculine journey. Actually, he has been trying to do that for some time now. You can choose to give up the false self, and walk away from the Woman as the one who validates you—or God can bring it all down. The choice is yours.

The history of a man's relationship with God is the story of how God calls him out, takes him on a journey, and gives him his true name. God's initiation of a man must take a very cunning course; he will wound us in the very place where we have been wounded. If we would walk with him in our initiatory journey, we must walk away from the false self—set it down, give it up willingly. Because so many of us turned to the Woman for our sense of masculinity, we must "walk away" from her as well—only in the sense that you stop asking her to validate you as a man. (I urge you to ask your wife to read through *Wild at Heart* on her own. I know—it's going to raise a lot of questions and expectations on her part, but this is so revolutionary that she's got to know what you are doing and *why*.)

We *desperately* need to know our name. So much else hangs on this— our sense of mission, or purpose in life, our ability to fight for others, and especially our impact on those we love most. I don't mean *know* in the way we "know" about the Battle of Waterloo or the ozone layer. I mean *know* in the deep, personal, firsthand experience way. Over the course of your Christian life, how would you classify your knowledge of God . . . and of yourself?

To speak of finding our true name is to describe that process whereby we shed the old identity for a new one; with that new identity comes a deeper strength, a life mission, a sense of self given to us by God. And yes, it may be embodied in an actual name . . . or it may be contained in a series of new "names" or phrases, such as "one who fights for the truth" or "tender warrior."

Most of us have been misinterpreting life and what God is doing for a long time. Before reading this chapter, what would you say God has been up to in your life over these past few years—I mean, how would you describe his activity or nonactivity in your life?

And what are the questions you've been asking God? What has been the subject of your prayers, that is, before reading *Wild at Heart*?

INITIATION

Where can you go to learn your true name, a name that can never be taken from you? That deep heart knowledge comes only through a process of *initiation*. The history of a man's relationship with God is the story of how God calls him out, takes him on a journey, and gives him his true name. Most of us have thought it was the story of how God sits on the throne waiting to whack a man broadside when he steps out of line. Not so. He created Adam for adventure, battle, and beauty; he created us for a unique place in his story, and he is committed to bringing us back to the original design. So God calls Abram out from Ur of the Chaldeans to a land he has never seen, to the frontier, and along the way Abram gets a new name. He becomes Abraham.

Even if your father did his job, he can only take you part of the way. There comes a time when you have to leave all that is familiar and go on into the unknown with God. Now let this question be from God to you: *Will you let me initiate you?*

To enter into a journey of initiation with God requires a new set of questions: What are you trying to teach me here? What issues in my heart are you trying to raise through this? What is it you want me to see?

Looking at our relationship with God in this way provides us with an entirely new orientation: God is initiating me. That gives us a whole new way of interpreting events, a new set of questions to be asking. How different would the past five years have been for you if you had seen them as a process of initiation, and asked those questions as all the things that have unfolded took place?

HOW YOU'VE HANDLED YOUR WOUND

God has been trying to initiate you for a long time. What is in the way is how you've mishandled your wound and the life you've constructed as a result. Most men *minimize* their wound . . .

➤ They deny it outright, or they
➤ Leave it in the past, or they
➤ Minimize the impact of the wound.

Other men may admit the wound but mishandle it because they *embrace* it or its message . . .

➤ "Yes, it was awful, but I deserved it," or
➤ "But what he said was true about me," or
➤ They take on a victim mentality and let the wound define them, embracing it to the point of needing the wound ("I'm weak . . . take care of me. And don't ever require me to be a man").

How have you handled your wound? And why did you choose that answer? Give a few examples.

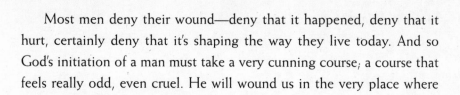
Most men deny their wound—deny that it happened, deny that it hurt, certainly deny that it's shaping the way they live today. And so God's initiation of a man must take a very cunning course; a course that feels really odd, even cruel. He will wound us in the very place where we have already been wounded.

THWARTING THE FALSE SELF

Okay, so now we have a new orientation—that God is initiating us, asking us on a mysterious and dangerous journey that will reveal to us our true name and our real place in his story. We also know that he does it by thwarting the false self and even wounding us in the place of our deepest wound. We also have a new set of questions to be asking "What issues in my heart are you trying to raise through this?" Do you have a pretty good hunch where God has been thwarting *you*? Why did you choose that?

What's basically been your plan for making life work, and why did you choose it? (Example: *Life will work out if I'm successful, and I chose that route because I'm good at making money but not good at much else.*)

How's it going? Is your plan working?

Where are you experiencing the most disappointment or "frustration" in your life?

Your career—how are things going there?

Your marriage (or pursuit of the Woman)—is it all you dreamed it would be?

And, if you have children, is everything terrific on that front?

Where in your life are you feeling vulnerable, or exposed, perhaps on shaky ground? Are you being asked to step into an arena you really fear?

What are you doing *in response* to those areas that aren't going that great? Are you scrambling to make it right? What are you hoping to remedy?

Where are you losing passion maybe giving up? Why?

Could it be that God is thwarting some aspect of your false self, thwarting some part of your plan for making life work? Why would he be closing in on that?

Every man has a plan for salvation, for making his life work. (Some of you are well on your way to repenting of that, and I'm cheering.) The plan is formed as a defense against the wound . . . and as an attempt to get some taste of what he was made for but in a way that's well within his control. That's why I said, "If we would walk with him in our journey of masculine initiation, we must walk away from the false self—set it down, give it up willingly. . . . We can choose to do it

ourselves, or we can wait for God to bring it all down." What do you
need to give up, walk away from, set down?

WALKING AWAY FROM THE WOMAN

As we walk away from the false self, we will feel vulnerable and
exposed. We will be sorely tempted to turn to our comforters for some
relief, those places that we've found solace and rest. Because so many
of us turned to the Woman for our sense of masculinity, we must walk
away from her as well. *I do not mean you leave your wife.* I mean you stop
looking to her to validate you, stop trying to get your answer from her.
If you've been a passive man, never doing anything to rock the boat,
then it's time to rock it. Stand up to her; get her mad at you. For those
of you violent men (including achievers), it means *you stop abusing her.*
You release her as the object of your anger. Repentance for a driven
man means you become *kind.* How have you handled the Woman in
your life? Why? For how long?

What does it mean for *you* to "walk away from the woman"?

A man needs a much bigger orbit than a woman. He needs a mission, a life purpose, and he needs to know his name. Only then does he have something to invite her into. What's your mission? What are you inviting your woman to join you in?

Ask your woman, "What could I do—or stop doing—that would feel like a great relief to you in our relationship?"

We only "walk away" from the Woman because we have some "soul work to do." What is the soul work you have to do?

The bottom line is this: We must reverse Adam's choice; we must choose God over Eve. We must take our ache to him, for only in God will we find the healing of our wound.

O God, I have tasted Your goodness, and it has both satisfied me and made me thirsty for more. I am painfully conscious of my need of further grace. I am ashamed of my lack of desire. O God, the Triune God, I want to want You; I long to be filled with longing; I thirst to be made more thirsty still. Show me Your glory, I pray You, that so I may know You indeed. Begin in mercy a new work of love within me. Say to my soul, "Rise up, my love, my fair one, and come away." Then give me grace to rise and follow You up from this misty lowland where I have wandered so long. In Jesus' name. Amen. (A. W. Tozer, The Pursuit of God)

CHAPTER 7

HEALING THE WOUND

*The deepest desire of our hearts is for union with God. God created
us for union with Himself. This is the original purpose of our lives.*
—BRENNAN MANNING

Our goal here is the healing of your wound, and the discovering of your
true name. It's the most important work in all the book, for every chapter
we've done thus far has led up to this, and every chapter that follows
relies upon the work of God here.

It's not a sign of weakness that you need God desperately—you were
meant to live in a deeply dependent relationship with him. The healing
of your wound begins by no longer despising those broken places within
you—after all, your wound was not your fault. You'll find the healing of
your masculine soul through a process that by its nature has to be very
personal—yet there are several phases that I lay out below. God has a
new name for us, and hearing that name is a deep part of the healing
process. That name reveals our true strength, our glory, and our
calling.

THOSE BROKEN PLACES WITHIN US

Most men, including myself, are embarrassed by their emptiness and
woundedness. We know we are meant to embody strength, we know
we are not what we were meant to be, and so we feel our brokenness
as a source of shame. How are you feeling about entering into your
wound?

Many men report feeling as though there is a boy inside, that something within them feels small and weak and fearful. Sadly, most of us despise that about ourselves, and we're harsh with the broken places within us. How have you treated your wounded heart, your brokenness?

Jesus said, "It would be better to be thrown into the sea with a large millstone tied around the neck than to face the punishment in store for harming one of these little ones" (Luke 17:2 NLT). God is *furious* about what's happened to you—he's not angry with you, he's angry *for* you. Think of how you would feel if the wounds you were given, the blows dealt to you, were dealt to a boy you loved. Would you shame him for it? Would you feel scorn that he couldn't rise above it all? What would you want for him?

All that happened—your father's wounding of you, the way the world emasculated you—none of that was your fault. Just stay with that sentence for a while; allow that to be true for you. *It's not your fault.* What rises in your heart?

How do you feel about needing help? Have you ever asked for help with your wound, your brokenness? Most of us are fiercely independent. What if receiving help was normal for a man, and meant nothing about failure or weakness?

ENTERING THE WOUND—THE DOORWAYS

Buechner was so right when he said that we bury our wound deep, and after a while we never take it out again, let alone speak of it. But take it out we must—or better, enter into it. . . . Christ must *touch* us, and touch us *where we hurt most*. There are many doorways God can use to take us back into our wound.

Dave sought his "healing" through the Woman; God took the Woman away. What has God taken away from you that has felt earthshaking? What has he thwarted, to get you into your wound?

My anger caused me to stop and look under the hood. That might be another door God uses. Ask yourself, *What's underneath the anger? Why am I so mad?*

Has a film or a song or a story brought you to tears, maybe for reasons you couldn't explain? Go back to that again; use it as a doorway for this journey.

Above all else, we offer a simple prayer:

Jesus, take me into my wound. I give you permission and access to my soul and to my deepest hurts. Come, and bring me to my own brokenness. Come and shepherd the orphaned boy within me. Let me be fully present to my wounded heart. Uncover my wound, and meet me there.

THE WAY OF HEALING

The way in which God heals our wound is a deeply personal process. For one man it happens in a dramatic moment; for another, it takes place over time. Even after we've experienced some real healing, God will often take us back again for a deeper work of healing. And so what I offer here is not a formula, but a way toward healing. You may want to bring this process to a man (preferably) or a woman who is known for his or her wisdom in the healing of the soul. Having someone walk with you through the restoration of your heart is something I strongly encourage.

SURRENDER

It all begins with surrender—that act of the will whereby we give ourselves back to God. So many of us have lived independently for so long—even men who call themselves Christians. Their faith has been more about practicing principles and maintaining morality than it has been about deep communion with God. May I recommend a prayer like this:

> *Dear Jesus, I am yours. You have ransomed me with your own life, bought me with your own blood. Forgive me for all my years of independence. I give myself back to you—all of me. I give my soul to you—my desperate search for life and love and validation. I give to you my spirit also, to be restored in union with you. Forgive me, cleanse me, take me and make me utterly yours. In your name I pray.*

RENOUNCE THE VOW

You'll remember that back in chapter 4 I described the vow many of us make after we are wounded—a vow that in some way protects us from ever being hurt again. The only thing more tragic than the tragedy that happens to us is the way we handle it—the choices we make, the person we become, the life we live (or don't live). The things we do to protect and preserve our hearts usually end up hurting us more.

You must renounce that vow deliberately, and out loud. The vow is a kind of *agreement* with the lie. . . . Breaking the vow is your way of canceling all agreements with the lie and taking back any ground you gave to the Enemy. It releases your soul for Christ to come in. This is something *you* must do, for Christ will not violate your will.

> *Jesus, I renounce every vow I've made to seal off my wound and protect myself from further pain. Reveal to me what those vows were. [If you can name them specifically, do so, and renounce them.] I break every agreement I have made*

with the lies that came with my wounds, the lies of Satan, and I make all agreement with you, Jesus. I give the protection of my heart and soul back to you, trust you with all that is within me. In your name I pray.

INVITATION

And then we invite Jesus into our wound, ask him to come and meet us there, to enter into the broken and unhealed places of our hearts and make us whole. All our healing and all our strength flows from our union with Christ.

And precious Jesus, I invite you into the wounded places of my heart, give you permission to enter every broken place. Come, dear Lord, and meet me there. Release my heart from every form of captivity and from every form of bondage. Restore and set free my heart, my soul, my mind, and my strength. Help me to mourn, and comfort me as I do. O come to me, Jesus, and surround me with your healing presence. Restore me through union with you. I ask in your name.

WE GRIEVE

It is so important for us to grieve our wound; it is the only honest thing to do. For in grieving we admit the truth—that we were hurt by someone we loved, that we lost something very dear, and it hurt us very much. Tears are healing. They help to open and cleanse the wound. As Augustine wrote in his *Confessions*, "The tears . . . streamed down, and I let them flow as freely as they would, making of them a pillow for my heart. On them it rested." Grief is a form of validation; it says the wound *mattered.*

Yes, Jesus—I confess that it mattered. It mattered deeply. Come into my soul and release the grief and tears bottled up within me. Help me to grieve my own wounds and sorrows.

Grief often has to sneak up on us, because we are so reluctant to allow it expression. Simply let it show up when it chooses to. Allow the tears to come out when they do begin to come.

WE LET GOD LOVE US

To be loved is to be hurt. That's why loving and being loved is a sign of great courage and strength. After all, Jesus loved us right up to the point of his own death. As John said at the Last Supper, "Having loved his own who were in the world, he now showed them the full extent of his love" (John 13:1). The most manly of us all was the most loving.

And as for needing love, again we find in Jesus something really surprising. What he most deeply craves, what he talks about with deepest delight is the Father's love and delight in him. This isn't a source of embarrassment to Christ; quite the opposite. He brags about his relationship with his Father. He's happy to tell anyone who will listen, "The Father and I are one" (John 10:30 NLT). They are intimate; they delight in each other.

Abiding in the love of God is our only hope, the only true home for our hearts. It's not that we mentally acknowledge that God loves us. It's that we let our hearts come home to him, and stay in his love.

> *Father, strengthen me with your true strength, by your Spirit in my innermost being, so that Jesus may live intimately in my heart. O let me be rooted and grounded in love, so that I, too, with all your precious saints, may know the fullness of the love of Jesus for me—its height and depth, its length and breadth. Let me be filled with real knowing of your love—even though I will never fully reason it or comprehend it—so that I might be filled with all the life and power you have for me. Do this in me, beyond all that I am able to ask or imagine.*

And then we *allow it to be true* that he does love us—we hold that truth in our hearts before we feel anything. God has loved you with an everlasting love. . . . We *stay* with that truth. . . . We let it linger in our hearts and minds throughout the days ahead—no matter what else occurs to us or happens around us.

FORGIVENESS

The time has come for us to forgive our fathers. For what? You know better than I. For the wound—or wounds. For the ways he failed you. For things he did and said *and* for things he did *not* do and did *not* say. Forgiveness is far more real and meaningful when we are specific about what we are forgiving. Write down these things. Your list doesn't need to be pages in length, but it does need to include the major blows.

This is an act of the will—not a feeling. Quite often the feelings come sometime later. And remember—forgiving is not saying, *It doesn't really matter;* it is not saying, *I probably deserved part of it anyway.* Forgiveness says, *It was wrong, it mattered, and I release you.*

> *Jesus, I choose to forgive my father for all the pain and all the wounds he gave to me. [It will help to be specific here.] It was wrong, it hurt me deeply, and I choose now to pardon him, because your sacrifice on the cross was enough to pay for these sins. I release my father to you. I also release any bitterness I've harbored toward him, and I ask you to come and cleanse these wounds and heal them. In your name I pray.*

OUR NEW NAME

Then we ask God to be our Father, and to tell us our true name. You must ask God what he thinks of you, what he sees in you, and you must *stay* with the question until you get an answer.

> *Father, who am I to you? You are my true Father—my Creator, my Redeemer, and my Sustainer. You know the man you had in mind when you made me. You know my true name. O Father, I ask you to speak to me, to reveal to me*

my true strength and my real name. Father, I ask that you speak it not once,
but again and again so that I might really receive it. And grant me the courage
to receive what you say and the faith to believe it. In Jesus' name.

The battle is going to get intense here. The Enemy, the Accuser, is
not going to take this one lying down. This is the last thing he wants
you to know. God may speak something immediately to you, and then
confirm it over time with other "new names" and revelations of who you
truly are as a man. Hang in there—this is part of your warrior training.

ON HEARING GOD'S VOICE

God "speaks" to us in many ways. First, there is his written word—
the Bible. He spoke to us in black and white because we needed
something rock-solid to build on. What *has* God said? A lot: You are my
true son (1 John 3:1). You are completely forgiven and cleansed (1 John
1:9). You have a new name (Isa. 62:2; Rev. 2:17).

We also know that God speaks to us through the body of Christ.
Men and women can help you hear your name, or validate the name
you've heard God speak to you personally.

God *does* speak to us intimately and personally as well. He speaks
through movies and songs and life experiences. He speaks through
dreams. And most of all, he speaks in our hearts for that is where
Christ dwells (Eph. 3:17). And he will speak to you through your *heart's*
desires. Who is the man you *want* to be? What is the battle you want
to have? That is your desire because that is who you *are*!! Go ahead—
embarrass yourself. What would you really love for God to say to you?

Do you know the hardest part of hearing your new name? Accepting it. Because the enemy arranges for our wound in a very specific, targeted way, it will help to reveal our calling and name. What has the wound prevented you from doing, or from trying, or from becoming over the years? This is a deep clue to who you really are.

The false self is never wholly false. What we do, you see, is find a few of our gifts and then live off them and hide everything else. It's a false self in that it's not a full self, a full picture of who you are.

Of course, all this means that we *reject the lie* as well, those deep lies that came in with our wound. No matter how true they might feel, God says they are lies. You are not alone; you are not a failure. Your new name is going to collide head-on with the lie that has been with you for a long time. Which are you going to believe? Better, *who* are you going to believe—the One you made you, or the father of lies?

As God does speak, WRITE IT DOWN. The Enemy will rush in and try to steal it or just make you forget. Keep coming back to it, rereading what God gave you, and adding to it as he gives you more!

Dearest Jesus, thank you for this great work you have begun in my heart. O take me deeper, Lord, deeper into healing, deeper into strength, deeper into my true name. Seal this work in my heart with your blood, and let not one ounce be stolen from me. Carry me on, I pray in your name. Amen.

CHAPTER 8

A BATTLE TO FIGHT: THE ENEMY

If we would endeavor, like men of courage, to stand in the battle, surely we would feel the favorable assistance of God from heaven. For he who giveth us occasion to fight, to the end we may get the victory, is ready to succor those that fight manfully, and do trust in his grace.

—THOMAS À KEMPIS

Over the next four chapters we are shifting from the healing of your masculine heart to the *release* of your heart into the Battle, the Adventure, and the Beauty. But we're going to start with the Battle because (1) it's where most men get taken out *and* (2) if you want the Beauty and the Adventure, you're going to have to fight for them! Our aim here is three-fold: to recover our warrior heart, to uncover the Enemy and his tactics, and to learn some strategy for winning this war.

A man must have a battle to fight, a great mission for his life that involves but also transcends home and family. God *has* given you a place in the Great Battle, and your initiation journey *will* take you there. As a warrior, you must have *vision* and *cunning*. To beat the enemy called the flesh, you must embrace the promise of the New Covenant—that God has given you a new heart. To beat the enemy of the world, you must expose the counterfeits it offers you—counterfeit battles, adventures, and beauties. And as for Satan . . . you begin by bringing him back into your real beliefs and the way you evaluate life.

Do you truly believe, down in your gut, that God has called you to a crucial front line and that you have the warrior heart required for the battle? If the answer is *yes!* tell me who gave that to you. If the answer is *no*, or *I have my doubts*, tell me who told you that.

Earlier in the book I said that the reason the Enemy fired all those arrows at your heart is *because he fears you*. Can you allow for a moment that that might be true? What does that possibility arouse in you?

Think about the films that you love. How many of them are stories of ordinary guys—underdogs, really—who finally step up into their true strength and engage? How many of the biblical stories are also "underdog" themes?

When the angel of the Lord saluted Gideon as a mighty warrior, do you know who Gideon was and what he happened to be doing? Gideon was—at least in his own eyes—a loser from the biggest family of losers, the youngest lad in a family known for its weakness. And he was at that moment threshing his wheat down in a hole, terrified of even being *noticed* by his enemies. There there is King David, who faced more battles and killed more men in hand-to-hand combat than we can count. The fierce warrior describes himself in the psalms as a "leaning wall" and a "tottering fence" about to fall over with the next strong wind (Ps. 62:3). It's just possible that your own self-estimation may not be very accurate, either.

There is no other man who can replace you in your life, in the arena you've been called to. If you leave your place in the line, it will remain empty. If you do not step up into the battle God has for you, who will take your place?

WARRIORS AND MERCENARIES

We could probably divide all the guys in the world up into three categories: (1) guys who have no battle, (2) guys who have a battle but it's the wrong one (King Saul trying to kill David), and (3) guys who truly know their place in the Battle.

Mercenaries are guys who are hired to fight, guys who have no stake in the battle at hand except a paycheck. They are fighting the wrong battle or for the wrong reason, or both. Saul thought he was fighting the right battle before that little incident on the Damascus road. And King Saul (is it something in the name?!) was certain it was his God-given mission to kill David. If you feel that you are in the right battle, are you willing to test that a bit? What is it over? What's at stake? Who called you to this battle? Who is your adversary?

How desperately do you need God to show up for any chance of victory? Is that how you pray about it? Really?

If you win the battles you are currently fighting, what will be the result? What will that bring *you*?

God created you to be his intimate *ally*, to join him in the Great Battle. You have a specific place in the line, a mission God made you for. That is why it is so essential to hear from God about your true name, because in that name is the mission of your life. Churchill was called upon to lead the British through the desperate hours of World War II. He said, "I felt as if I were walking with destiny, and that all my past life had been but a preparation for this hour and for this trial." The same is true of you. Do you have any sense of what that preparation has been, and what your Great Battle might be?

What issue gets you riled up, makes you pound your fist on the table? And what does that issue represent to you?

OUR ENEMY—THE FLESH

Having a vision is only part of our warrior training. The second quality of a warrior's life is *cunning*—knowing when to fight and when to run, knowing what weapons to use and when. . . . How would you live if you knew that there was a group of terrorists sent into the U.S. to take you out? That's the mentality that breeds a kind of daily cunning.

We'll start with the flesh, partly because that tends to be the only enemy the church talks about much. Remember, when I use the term *flesh* I am referring not to our physical body but to our "sin nature." How would you describe your own "flesh" these days? Who is the poser that is your "flesh"?

Do you have a growing awareness of how your flesh would like to betray you—or sabotage your strength—when it comes to . . .

The Battle?

The Adventure?

The Beauty?

THE NEW HEART

Okay, now for one of the biggest issues we'll ever come to terms with, as big as our wound or our new name or even facing the enemy. Is your flesh the real you? Are you a sinner at the core? What have you been taught about that?

Man in his fallen state, man separated from God, has a wicked heart. But in Jeremiah 31:31–33, God promises to remedy the condition of the human heart with a brand-new arrangement. And in Ezekiel 36:26–27 God reiterates that promise of a new covenant, a new arrangement with mankind. So what exactly is the promise of the New Covenant? How does God plan to deal with the fallen human heart?

The New Testament is the record of God keeping his promise. It details the New Covenant he offers to man and all that means for our lives. In his writings especially, Paul lays out slowly and clearly the doctrine of the New Covenant and what Christ has accomplished for us (see Romans 6:8–11; 2 Corinthians 5:21; Colossians 2:11). Christ's righteousness is now ours.

What about our sin? Don't we still face a battle against the flesh? Indeed we do. But you can't hope to win that battle if you believe that your flesh is the real you, that you are still by nature a sinner. Paul wrote, "I know that nothing good lives in me, *that is, in my sinful nature.* For I have the desire to do what is good, but I cannot carry it out. For what I do is not the good I want to do; no, the evil I do not want to do—this I keep on doing. Now if I do what I do not want to do, *it is no longer I who do it, but it is sin living in me that does it*" (Rom. 7:18–20, emphasis added). What distinction is Paul making here about his true desires and his sinful nature?

Paul also wrote, "I pray that out of [God's] glorious riches he may strengthen you with power through his Spirit in your inner being, so that Christ may dwell in your hearts through faith" (Eph. 3:16–17). Where does Christ dwell in a man who believes in him? And is it possible that the part of our heart which Christ dwells in is evil?

There is only one conclusion we can draw from the New Covenant and all God has done for us in and through Christ. The real you is on the side of God against the false self. Knowing this makes all the difference in the world. How would believing that your true heart *is* for God, and *is* one with Christ, and therefore *is* good . . . how would that change the way you approach life?

Your flesh is your *false self* and the only way to deal with it is to crucify it. Now follow me very closely here: We are never, ever told to crucify our heart. We are never told to kill the true man within us, never told to get rid of those deep desires for battle and adventure and beauty. We are told to shoot the traitor. How? Choose against him every time you see him rouse his ugly head. Speak right to the issues you normally remain silent over. If you want to grow in true masculine strength, then you must stop sabotaging yours. Do you ever speak up in a meeting at work or at church? It's time to speak up. Do you ever ask your wife how she's feeling, even though you have no idea what to do with what she might say? It's time to ask her. How else can you stop sabotaging and start letting your strength arrive?

LETTING OUR STRENGTH SHOW UP

We must let our strength show up. It seems so strange, after all this, that a man would not allow his strength to arrive, but many of us are unnerved by our own masculinity. What will happen if we really let it out? What do you *fear* will happen?

One thing we know. Nothing will ever be the same. What might change if you really let your masculine heart and your true strength show up . . .

At work?

At home?

At church?

OUR ENEMY—THE WORLD

The world is a carnival of counterfeits—counterfeit battles, counterfeit adventures, counterfeit beauties. Where have you been suckered by the world in the past? And where do you hear it seducing you nowadays?

Men should think of it as a corruption of their strength. The world offers a man a false sense of power and security. Where does your sense of power come from most of the time? Is it how well you're doing, or what you know, or what others think of you?

Where do you feel strongly pulled to turn for a sense of validation as a man? What is calling to you, promising you that?

We should let people feel the weight of who we are, and let them deal with it. By that I do not mean we become belligerent or recklessly destructive with our current situation. What I mean is that we come out from hiding, stop apologizing that we have a wild heart, stop editing ourselves to fit neatly within a world of posers. Many things are probably calling for a change. Much of our present life was built by and for a poser, and when the poser changes, his world will change as well. But remember that a warrior uses *cunning*. Pick your battles.

The world of posers is shaken by a real man. They'll do whatever it takes to get you back in line—threaten you, bribe you, seduce you, undermine you. They crucified Jesus. But it didn't work, did it? You must let your strength show up. Remember Christ in the Garden of Gethsemane, the sheer force of his presence? When you let your strength show up, what do you expect the reaction is going to be . . .

At work?

At home?

At church?

And what about a false sense of security? Consider what you would think of yourself if tomorrow you lost everything that the world has rewarded you for. What do you fear losing, and what would you feel about yourself if you did lose it all?

THE DEVIL

Now for the enemy we have been taught the least about—Satan. Does Satan have any place in your actual thinking? What event in your life, what arrow or temptation, what thought or occurrence have you attributed to him this week? This month? This year? Name five things.

How about your work here in this field manual—has everything been going smoothly? No fears, no confusion, no doubts? Has Satan been at work at all against you here?

Strengthen me, with your strength, O God. Rally my soul into this great battle. Dear Jesus, expose the enemies of my heart and my life so that I may see the battle lines more clearly. Show me my place, speak again to me my name. Grant me a vision for my life, and grant me the cunning of a warrior. Sustain me in this battle and in this journey, that in your name I might gain the victory. I pray in the mighty power of Jesus' name. Amen.

CHAPTER 9

A BATTLE TO FIGHT: THE STRATEGY

As part of Christ's army, you march in the ranks of gallant spirits. Every one of your fellow soldiers is the child of a King. Some, like you, are in the midst of battle, besieged on every side by affliction and temptations. Others, after many assaults, repulses, and rallyings of their faith, are already standing upon the wall of heaven as conquerors. From there they look down and urge you, their comrades on earth, to march up the hill after them. This is their cry: "Fight to the death and the City is your own, as now it is ours!"

—WILLIAM GURNALL

In the masculine journey a man needs three things: (1) He needs to get his heart back. (2) He needs to know his place in the battle. (3) He needs to know how to fight. Your goal here is learning something of #3—how to fight in a spiritual war.

Stage One of Satan's strategy is always "I'm not here—this is just you." Most men live their whole lives duped at that level. In Stage Two Satan moves to intimidation—trying to threaten us back in line. At Stage Three he offers us a deal of some kind. We've been given our aggressive heart to fight aggressively. And God has provided the weapons we need. The kingdom of heaven suffers violence, and violent men take it by force.

STAGE ONE: "I'M NOT HERE"

What was your reaction to the true story from D-day, about the paratroopers who hid themselves in a farmhouse and got drunk on the night of one of the most important battles in the history of mankind?

These men *knew* they were at war, yet they refused to act like it. They lived in a dangerous denial that not only endangered them but countless others who depended on them to do their part. I believe it is a *perfect* picture of the Western church when it comes to spiritual warfare. Do you think I exaggerate? Name three men you know who take Satan seriously—who talk openly about his schemes and who pray out loud directly against him on a regular basis.

Both Peter and James commented on the devil. Peter wrote, "Be self-controlled and alert. Your enemy the devil prowls around like a roaring lion looking for someone to devour. *Resist him*, standing firm in the faith" (1 Peter 5:8–9, emphasis added), and James wrote, "Submit yourselves, then, to God. *Resist the devil*, and he will flee from you" (James 4:7, emphasis added). What is God saying through Peter and James that we must do in our battle against the devil? Which part of your heart does that engage, call up?

The Enemy always tries to jam the lines of communication. Do you ever experience that sense of *accusation* in your marriage or key friendships, that feeling that you're just not measuring up?

What about during prayer—are you able to focus without any interruptions? Do this exercise today or tomorrow: Notice every thought that interferes or distracts or discourages or condemns. What do you discover? Write it down.

Many, many times I've come under a cloak of *confusion* so thick I suddenly find myself wondering why I ever believed in Jesus in the first place. That sweet communion I normally enjoy with God is cut off, gone. If you don't know what's up, you'll think you really have lost your faith or been abandoned by God or whatever spin the Enemy puts on it. Has that ever happened to you? Does it happen on a regular basis? Has it happened at any point during your work through this manual? Who did you blame that on?

Satan is constantly putting his spin on things. Oh, if we would see this more clearly, what freedom it would bring! Do you find yourself coming to conclusions about what another person is thinking or feeling toward you? Write down what you think your wife, your boss, or your closest friend thinks about you these days, then ask yourself, *Has that person actually said that to me, or is that just what I kind of "sense" is going on?*

Wife

Boss

Friend

Satan is called the accuser of the brethren (Rev. 12:10) for a reason. His deepest and most crippling attacks are always accusations against our hearts, our identities, our new names. We've *got* to see this more clearly, expose it. Think of what goes on—what you hear and feel—when you really blow it. Recall a recent event . . . write down what you normally just let play through your head. (Examples: *I'm such an idiot, I always do that, I'll never amount to anything.*)

How about when you're really going to step forward as a man? What kind of accusation did you hear (are you hearing now)?

What are the sentences about yourself that you've been hearing for years? How have you felt, in a personal way, that *your heart is bad and you know it?*

We've got to stop making agreements with the Enemy. Satan will come looking for a weakness in our defenses. What agreements have you been making with the Enemy's lies? Can you name them?

Break those agreements now.

Dear Jesus, forgive me for making these agreements with the Enemy. I break those agreements now [name them] and I renounce the lie. You are the Way and the Truth and the Life; all the ground that I once gave to Satan I now give to you and you alone. In the authority of your name I pray. Amen.

HANGING ON TO THE TRUTH

You're just not going to be able to live an ordinary life anymore. I'm sorry. But you know too much now. You are too dangerous to leave alone, and the Enemy is going to come after you, to try to put you back in your place.

The battle can get ugly. He'll do everything he can to get you to think and feel as if what he says is the bottom-line truth. *But this is where your strength is revealed and increased through exercise.* Stand on what is true and do not let go. Period. No matter what you may feel.

You need to start swinging back. Right now, right here, I want you to write down what is true about you according to Scripture and according to those personal words God has spoken to you. Who are you, *really?*

Please don't misunderstand me. It may sound as if I'm blaming everything on the devil. I'm not. Nor do I want you to. C. S. Lewis said there are two mistakes the church makes when dealing with the devil: to blame everything on him or to blame nothing on him. Do neither.

Bottom Line: We answer Satan's Stage One with "You are here, and I'm sick of you blaming everything on me. I am onto your schemes."

STAGE TWO: INTIMIDATION

The next level of the Enemy's strategy is intimidation. When we begin to question him, to resist his lies, then he steps up the attack; he turns to intimidation and fear. He moves from subtle seduction to open assault. Has anything gone wrong in your life since you began work in this manual? What happened? Did you see the Enemy's hand in it? How have you responded?

REALLY?

What can Satan cause, I mean, really? Most men would admit that the devil is probably behind some of the temptation and maybe the accusation in their lives. But that's about it. Let's look at what the Bible says.

PHYSICAL AFFLICTION

There's the story of the woman in the synagogue who couldn't even stand up straight, "who had been crippled by a spirit" (Luke 13:11). And dare we forget Job, who experienced "painful sores" as a direct result of Satan's attack (Job 2:7). Jesus healed a mute boy and a blind man *by kicking out a demon* (Mark 9:14–26; Matt. 12:22).

FINANCIAL AFFLICTION

Who was behind the Chaldean raid on Job's herds, an event that wiped him out financially? Satan, clearly (Job 1:12, 17).

SPIRITUAL DOUBT, DISCOURAGEMENT, DISBELIEF

Paul says that Satan has "blinded the minds of unbelievers" (2 Cor. 4:4). But his work doesn't stop with non-Christians. Acts 5 recounts the story of Ananias and Sapphira, believers whose hearts were moved by Satan to lie to the elders of their church. . . . Daniel 10 tells the story of how an angel of God was delayed *three weeks* from getting through to Daniel because of spiritual warfare! I'll bet Daniel just thought his prayers weren't effective (see Daniel 10:1–14).

RELATIONAL DISTRESS AND CONFLICT

I'm really surprised at the number of men who think that this battle is going to be easy. They wonder why the Enemy doesn't run away at the first sign of our resistance. Yes, Scripture says that if we resist the devil, he will flee from us (James 4:7). And he will, but there is sometimes quite a battle wrapped up in that word *resist*. All that *aggression* God put in you this is what it's for—aggressive spiritual warfare.

There's the man in the synagogue possessed by an evil spirit, who starts shouting that Jesus is the Holy One of God. Jesus has to rebuke him in a stern voice (Luke 4:35). Good grief—if Jesus had to get downright aggressive . . . do you think we'll need to say more than a quick prayer?

Bottom Line: Our answer to Satan for Stage Two is, "I'm not giving up and I'm not going away. *You* are the one that has to flee."

STAGE THREE: CUTTING A DEAL

After a round or two of intimidation, Satan then offers us a deal. He'll "suggest" to you through thoughts and feelings—sometimes through the words of another person—that your life would be easier if you just backed off. Maybe you've heard or thought something like this: *I don't know about all this spiritual warfare stuff. This seems a little extreme. I think I'll just focus on the Adventure.*

Has the Enemy offered you a deal you've been able to identify?

Bottom Line: Our answer to Stage Three is, "No deals. My heart and my loyalty belong to God. I am in this for the duration."

THE WEAPONS OF WAR

This is a real war we're talking about. Men have been taken out right and left. "Do not be afraid of what you are about to suffer. I tell you, the devil will put some of you in prison to test you, and you will suffer persecution for ten days. Be faithful, even to the point of death, and I will give you the crown of life" (Rev. 2:10). If you want to survive, better still, if you want to *prevail*, you're going to need several things.

INTIMACY WITH GOD

Most men have a hard time sustaining any sort of devotional life because it has no vital connection to recovering and protecting their strength. On a scale of 1 to 10, with 1 being the thrill of flossing and 10 being great sex, where would you put your devotional life?

We do not give a halfhearted attempt at the spiritual disciplines because we ought to; we do it because *we are history if we don't*. We've got to keep those lines of communication open. Can you think of some times in the past that were rich with God? What were you doing?

Do *that* for your devotions.

INTIMACY WITH OTHERS

Don't even *think* about going into battle alone. Don't even try to take the masculine journey without at least one man by your side. We don't need accountability groups; we need *fellow warriors*. Name one or two guys whom you'd want to gather with to fight for each other. Will you approach them and raise the idea?

THE ARMOR OF GOD

Okay, God has given you the armor. Wear it. Daily. Start by praying it on, as I laid out on page 173 in *Wild at Heart*.

THE AUTHORITY OF CHRIST

ALL of our victory in this life comes through what Christ has already accomplished for us in his death, his resurrection, and his ascension. I've used daily prayers over the years to take my place in Christ, in his cross, resurrection, and ascension, and gain the victory over the Enemy. Find a daily prayer (or prayers) that works for you—whether it's your own or one that someone else has written—and make it a point to pray it. For example, one that I use is "Saint Patrick's Breastplate" and another is one I found in Ed Murphy's *The Spiritual Warfare Handbook*.

"The kingdom of heaven suffers violence," said Jesus, "and violent men take it by force" (Matt. 11:12 NASB). Things are going to get fierce. That's why you were given a fierce heart. Do you have something better to do with your life?

Pray your daily prayer now.

CHAPTER 10

A BEAUTY TO RESCUE

Beauty is not only a terrible thing, it is also a mysterious thing. There God and the Devil strive for mastery, and the battleground is the heart of men.

—DOSTOYEVSKY

Most of you will have a woman in your life—your wife, the woman you hope will be your wife, or a woman you are thinking of pursuing. Yes, God does call a few men to singleness—but only a few. For most of us, the Battle for the Beauty is core to our masculine journey. So the goal here is to engage that fight for her more clearly and willfully than we ever have before.

Your woman has been asking one question, too, ever since she was young, *Am I lovely?* And now the damsel is in distress; she, too, has been wounded in her heart. If you ever hope to truly enjoy the Beauty, you are going to have to *fight* for her. It's a battle that takes time. The tower comes down one brick at a time. You offer your strength for her in order to heal her wound, to help answer *her* Question with a resounding *YES*. But in this battle you cannot take *your* Question to her. Win or lose, this is about the kind of man you want to be.

THE BEAUTY WE LONG FOR

Okay, let's admit it—this is the deepest and hardest battle we ever face. The tower is real, the damsel is in distress, and the dragon isn't going to roll over and say, "Sure—take her. Live happily ever after." What is more, this battle cuts to the quick of our own masculinity more than any other. . . . We've all stayed clear of this battle *for a reason*. Am I right? What are you feeling as you think of fighting for your wife's heart, going to a whole new level in your relationship?

Bottom line is, you've got to be *compelled*, you've got to be gripped in a deep way if you're going in and staying in on this one. Think about the rest of your days with the Eve in your life—what do you *want* with her? What are you hoping to come out with on the other side?

What do you want sexually with her?

What do you want emotionally with her?

What do you want spiritually with her?

EVE'S HEART

It would be good to begin with a refresher on the heart of a woman. Reread pages 16–17 and 36–37 in the book. What was your woman designed to desire? (She may not act like she desires those things, or anything at all, but stay with the *design* of the feminine heart.)

Can you name a woman you've known who embodies those feminine desires? Do you have a good picture of a truly alive woman? Who is she?

What does it feel like to be around your wife, or your woman? Is she *alluring, vulnerable, inviting*? Or do you experience her as just *busy*, maybe *controlling*—or perhaps *clingy, demanding*? Choose a handful of words that describe your woman.

If she could become a woman you'd be thrilled to be married to, what would she be? Describe her. What is a truly beautiful woman to you . . .

In the bedroom?

Outside the bedroom?

And what would it do for you if in a year or two your woman looks into your eyes and says, "You have given me something I never thought possible. You've fought for me so amazingly, you've given me such adventure, and I know I am beautiful because of you. Come and enjoy my beauty"? Does the thought of that arouse you, or is it so far from your current reality it simply seems unreachable?

And what does your answer to that question say to you about what you've done with your heart, as far as your beauty is concerned? Are you "rarin' to go," hopeful, longing but doubtful, cynical?

EVE'S WOUND

The deep cry of a little girl's heart is, *Am I lovely?* Every woman needs to know that she is exquisite and exotic and *chosen.* This is core to her identity, the way she bears the image of God. Do you see this core longing in her life today? How? Where? If not, what does that tell you about what's happened to her heart?

She's been wounded, just like you. . . . Like your wound, hers probably came from her father. Do you know what your wife's wound is, and how it came? Has she ever told you about it? Have you ever asked? If not, do you have a hunch what the message given to her by her father was? How did he speak to her heart's deepest Question?

It would be a gift to help your wife understand her wound, and how it came, and how it's shaped her as a woman. For starters, after she's read the chapter, you might suggest the following explorations. With them and other questions below, I suggest you first offer them to her for her own reflection. Later, it would be wonderful if she could trust you with this information.

What are some of your favorite memories together with your dad? *Why* are they favorite memories?

Can you recall a time as a little girl when you felt deeply *delighted* in by your father? What happened?

If you did experience delight, or maybe just approval from your father, what was that for? Was it achievements of some kind? Good grades, or good behavior?

Would you say your father was a violent man, a driven man, a hesitant and passive man, or a dead man?

What *is* your heart's deepest wound as a woman? Can you put words to it? Do you remember how it was given?

And what was the *message* of that wound—or that series of wounds? What did it say to you about yourself as a woman?

Do you have a sense of how that wound is affecting you today?

To understand your wife's feminine journey, you must also under-stand her history with men—just as you explored in chapter 5 your history with women.

What has been your history with men? List the names of the key men in your life, the men you've had a relationship with or wanted a relationship with. Start with your first love, your first sweetheart, and go right up to the present, including your husband or current relationship. Then, answer the following questions for each man:

Who pursued whom?

What was the relationship like? Was it stormy, placid, passionate?

Who led during the course of the relationship?

How did he make you feel about yourself as a woman?

Who broke up with whom? What was the message to you?

What were you looking for from him? Do you see the way you took your Question to him?

Notice the flow of all your relationships—do you see a pattern emerging?

Do you see how it affected you?

What do you feel you're currently getting as a grade from your man? What does that make you want to go do?

YOUR PART IN THE WOUND

To battle for your wife, you'll need to know not only what her childhood wound was, but also how you've contributed to it. . . . What kind of man did your wife marry when she married you?

Did either of you understand your own wounds at that time?

Why did you marry your wife? Was it to offer your strength, rescue her heart, sweep her up into a great adventure? Or was it more about safety, or your own search for validation, or sexual satisfaction?

Most romances end up with evenings in front of the TV. Where are you today? Passionate pursuit? Comfortable safety? Volatile anger or distant withdrawal?

What have you communicated to her over the years about her deepest Question? Have your words, and more important, your actions, told her in a thousand ways, *Yes, you are lovely and worth fighting for?* Give a few examples for why you say yes, or no.

Once you have some understanding of her own life story, her wound, and the pattern that developed with men over the years, can you see how you've played right into the Enemy's hand—how you've added to her wound, to the patterns, or at best, how little you've done to heal them intentionally, with understanding?

OFFERING YOUR STRENGTH

We offer our strength to tear down the walls of the tower and speak to her heart's deepest Question in a thousand ways. We offer our words and actions to express our delight in her.

Let's start with *words*. Your woman craves words from you, longs for conversation with you. Offer it. This is not going to kill you. How many times a week do you tell your wife that you love her? That she is lovely, or pretty?

In a given week, is it common for the two of you to have a personal conversation about your life or hers, one that lasts more than five minutes?

There's no formula for this, but if you're not speaking to her heart's desire to be delighted in daily, if intimate conversations are less than weekly, you're starving her. Ante up, brother.

Now let's look at your *actions*:

How often do you offer your wife physical attention without expecting it to lead to sex?

Again, if it's less than daily you've got your mission laid out right there.

Have you given her flowers, a card, a gift, taken her to dinner or on a getaway trip *for no reason whatsoever?*

These sorts of things should occur several times a year at least.

What sort of sacrifices have you made this year to demonstrate to your wife that she is your priority?

What would feel really threatening to you right now in terms of what you could do to move toward your wife? What would feel really risky?

THE ENEMY

Don't forget there's a dragon. Heads up. What has the Enemy used against you in the past, when it comes to your woman?

And what are the truths you will use to fight back against him as he comes the next time around?

TALKING ABOUT THIS WITH HER

This chapter—the whole book in fact—can be the turning point in a whole new level of love and redemption in your marriage. But it isn't going to be easy. You are going to have to fight for her over the long haul. And you're going to have to beware the arrows the Enemy will fire at you with increased anger because you're moving in this direction.

This is not a formula. *The words you use and the approach you take aren't nearly as important as your heart toward her.* I recommend starting with *your* heart toward her. Share with her what the book has meant to you, what God has been doing in your life through this study. Tell her about your wound and then ask about hers. Ask her how *you've* wounded her over the years. Listen without defending. Ask her what she wants with you in the years ahead.

Now listen, brother—if she is so courageous to go here with you and she shares her heart's desire with you, then you have been given a price-less treasure few men get. DO IT. Do exactly what she's asked.

ONE FINAL WORD

Every man I know has taken some painful wounds as he's tried to rescue the Beauty in his life. The spiritual warfare can get pretty intense, too. And you'll need to fight it as such. A warrior is in this for good.

Dear God, forgive me for living a selfish, self-protecting life. Forgive me for not spending my life on behalf of my woman, and for all the wounds I've given her. O grant me the grace to undo the damage and bring that tower down. Awaken me to the real battle for her, expose the Enemy and his tactics against her and against our marriage. Give me your fierce love, your jealous love for my wife and for her freedom. And grant me courage, cunning, and selflessness as I fight for her. I ask this in your name. Amen.

CHAPTER 11

AN ADVENTURE TO LIVE

The place that God calls you is the place where your deep gladness and the world's deep hunger meet.

—FREDERICK BUECHNER

Our goal here is to recover that adventure God wrote on your heart when he made you. Your deepest desires reveal your deepest calling, the adventure God has for you. You must decide whether or not you'll exchange a life of control born out of fear for a life of risk born out of faith. It's high time you get on with *that* story.

Life is not a problem to be solved; it is an adventure to be lived. Therefore, a man just won't be happy until he's got adventure in his work, his love, and his spiritual life. Yet most men sacrifice their dreams because of fear, and they live out a script someone else wrote for them. Your true calling is written on your true heart, and you'll discover it when you enter the frontier of your deep desires. Ultimately, this means you forsake a careful life that depends on formulas for an intimate, conversational walk with God.

MADE FOR ADVENTURE

I want you to recall some of the adventures you've had from the major seasons of your life. When did you *really* experience freedom, exhilaration, take a risk, come alive . . .

As a boy?

As a teen/young man?

As a grown man?

ASKING THE RIGHT QUESTION

I told the story of how I became an author and a counselor, how that journey began with these simple words:

Don't ask yourself what the world needs. Ask yourself what makes you come alive, and go do that, because what the world needs is people who have come alive.

Is that the question you asked yourself that led to the life *you* are living now? If not, what was the question you asked that resulted in the life you now have?

I found myself at a sort of crossroads: Down one road was my dream and desire, which I had no means to pay for and an absolutely uncertain future after that; down the other was a comfortable step up the ladder of success, a very obvious next career move and total loss of my soul. Have you ever stood at a crossroads like that? What did you do? Is that what your heart most wanted to do?

Too many men forsake their dreams because they aren't willing to risk, or fear they aren't up to the challenge, or are never told that those desires deep in their hearts are *good*. If you left some or even all your dreams by the side of the road, can you remember what motivated you to forsake your dreams? What might be blocking you from pursuing them still?

WHAT ARE YOU WAITING FOR?

Genesis makes it clear why we long for adventure, to hurl ourselves into a creative work worthy of God. It's why he made us.

God raised David up to be king over Israel, and to deliver them from their enemies. That was his destiny. What God *called* David to do was exactly what David *wanted* to do. Paul was called to be an apostle, and that's what he loved to do. No matter what town or situation he found himself in, he started doing apostle-like things. His calling was his desire. Nehemiah was called by God to rebuild the walls of Jerusalem, and that's what *his* heart ached to do.

Obviously, God is not the enemy of desire. Furthermore, he "gives" us our desires in two ways. He puts them in our heart, and then he fulfills them.

If you had permission to do what you really want to do, what would you do? Ask yourself what makes you come alive. Just start making a list of all the things you deeply desire to do with your life, great and small. *Don't ask yourself, How? How?* is never the right question. *How?* is God's department. He is asking you *what?* What is written on your heart?

I suggest you get away from the noise and distraction of your daily life for time with your own soul. Head into the wilderness, to silence and solitude. Allow whatever is there to come to the surface. Once you've made a list of the things you'd love to do with your life, look it over—do you see any *themes* emerging? Could you place an urgency on some desires over others? *This I'd love to do, but this I'll die if I never do.*

Sometimes our dreams are buried deep and it takes some unearthing to get to them. Often the clues are in our past. What did you most enjoy in school? What were your best moments?

When you walk into a bookstore, what section do you go to?

How about jobs you really loved, or, better assignments *within* a job that you truly enjoyed?

Were there some times in your life when people said, "Wow—you really impacted me"? What were you doing?

Warning!: Obviously, I am not suggesting that every desire we have is good, nor that every desire reflects God's will for us. As Paul said, "So I say, live by the Spirit, and you will not gratify the desires of the sinful nature" (Gal. 5:16).

Using the idea that Jesus is our Prophet, Priest, and King, I find that men tend to fall into one of those categories when it comes to their desires and their calling. *Kings* love to build, invest, create, and care for the realm. *Priests* love to care for people on a more personal basis. *Prophets* love to shake the system, to bring people back to the truth. Look over your desires list and your life survey. Do you see a Prophet, Priest, or King theme emerging?

Sometimes when we allow our soul a chance to come up for air, what we first encounter is *grief* for so much lost time. There, beneath the grief, are desires long forsaken. What are your deepest regrets about your life? What are the desires you abandoned?

INTO THE UNKNOWN

As you stand again at the crossroads, or what may feel like a *precipice*, you are going to face two obstacles to embracing the Adventure. Those obstacles are fear and mystery (or simply the unknown). Mystery is the heart of the universe and the God who made it. The most important aspects of your world—your relationship with God and with the people in your life, your calling, the spiritual battles— every one of them is fraught with mystery. What are the major fears you have as you embark on the adventures God is stirring in you?

What will you do with those fears and with the unknown? We have three choices—(1) to shrink back and reject the invitation to Adventure; (2) to try to reach for some sort of formula that will give us a sense of control; or (3) to simply venture forward with God. This is the moment your true strength begins to be released. What are you feeling tempted to do? Can you distinguish the voices of your false self, your Enemy, and your true heart?

Ultimately, we must take our fears to God, who is perfect love, and ask him to speak to them personally. Walking with him will always involve risk. That is why following God into the Adventures he has for us always comes down to, *Will you trust me?* For what he offers us is *himself.*

FROM FORMULA TO RELATIONSHIP

The problem with modern Christianity's obsession with principles is that it removes any real conversation with God. Find the principle, apply the principle—what do you need God for? Would you say your Christian life has been more oriented toward rules and regulations, or a personal relationship with God?

There are no formulas with God. Period. So there are no formulas for the man who follows him. God is a person, not a doctrine. The only way to live in this adventure is an ongoing, intimate relationship with God. I used Moses and Abraham and David as examples, but the danger in doing that is some men will say, "Well sure, that was true for them, but c'mon now—I'm just an ordinary guy, not a patriarch out of the Bible." Do you think that sort of conversational intimacy with God is available to you? What is your position based on—Scripture, or experience?

Learning to hear the voice of God in our hearts and recognize his hand in our lives is something that is *cultivated* over time. We grow into it; we learn to discern between our thoughts and his voice and the voice of the Enemy.

I always hear better when my heart has been tuned to Christ through worship, or devotional reading, or through silence and solitude. Tune your heart in first. Then ask your questions.

Lay your agenda on the altar. When God speaks in our hearts, the message will never contradict Scripture. The written Word of God is always our benchmark. Also, is it consistent with other things God has made clear to you over the years? Does it ring true with your new heart, with the Spirit of God within you? Finally, what is the effect of what you're hearing—does it rouse hope and require faith?

Last, when it comes to critical and crucial questions, ask God for a confirmation of what you have heard—a scripture that affirms it, or a word of counsel from a godly ally, or an event that sheds further light on the matter.

Our whole journey into authentic masculinity centers around those cool-of-the day talks with God. Simple questions change hassles into adventures; the events of our lives become opportunities for initiation. Do you sense what God is saying to you about those questions even now? Take an event that's unfolding right now in your life, and bring those questions to him about it.

FURTHER UP AND FURTHER IN

My guess is, the journey that now lies ahead of you doesn't seem real clear. Am I right? That's not a bad sign. The call of God always, *in every case*, requires deeper intimacy with God. All God usually reveals to us is a big vision, written in our desire, and the next couple of steps. Consider that an act of mercy. If he had told you all that was going to happen in your life up to *this* point, would you have really wanted to know?

Move on to chapter 12, and write the next chapter of your life.

I want to love with much more abandon and stop waiting for others to love me first. I want to hurl myself into a creative work worthy of you, God. I want to follow Peter as he followed you out onto the sea. Give me your great heart within me to live the adventure you have for me. In Jesus' name. Amen.

WRITING THE NEXT CHAPTER

> *Freedom is useless if we don't exercise it as characters making choices.*
> *. . . We are free to change the stories by which we live. Because we*
> *are genuine characters, and not mere puppets, we can choose our*
> *defining stories. We can do so because we actively participate in the*
> *creation of our stories. We are co-authors as well as characters. Few*
> *things are as encouraging as the realization that things can be dif-*
> *ferent and that we have a role in making them so.*
>
> —DANIEL TAYLOR

Now, reader, it is your turn to write—venture forth with God.

A BATTLE TO FIGHT

What great battle would you love to devote your life to? What do you
want to be different about the world or about the church or about
someone's life because you lived?

And what is the next move you need to make in order to move toward
that vision?

Will you do it? When?

AN ADVENTURE TO LIVE

What great adventure would you love to enter into? What quest would you love to take?

And what is the next move you need to make in order to move toward that vision?

Will you do it? When?

A BEAUTY TO RESCUE

Who is the woman God has called you to fight for? (Some of you won't have an answer for this right now. That's okay. This can apply to women in your family, female friends, or the woman who may one day come.) What is the impact you want your life to have upon hers?

And what is the next step you need to take in order to move toward her, fight for her?

Will you do it? When?

O God, dear Jesus thank you for the work you have done in my life thus far. Lord, all I can say is I want more! More courage, more conviction, more healing, more vision, more of you. Carry me on in this great Quest. When I falter, quicken me. When I fail, encourage me again. And as I move into my true strength and my true place in your great story, O God, all the praise and glory will be to you. I am in this for good. In Jesus' name. Amen.

You've come far enough now that this is about *you*, valiant one:

It is not the critic who counts; not the man who points out how the strong man stumbles, or where the doer of deeds could have done them better. The credit belongs to the man in the arena, whose face is marred by dust and sweat and blood; who strives valiantly . . . who knows the great enthusiasm, the great devotions; who spends himself in a worthy cause; who at the best knows in the end the triumph of high achievement, and who at the worst, if he fails, at least fails while daring greatly, so that his place shall never be with those cold and timid souls who have never known neither victory nor defeat.

—Teddy Roosevelt